mini ARCHITECTS

mini ARCHITECTS

20 projects inspired by the great architects

Joséphine Seblon

illustrated by Robert Sae-Heng

Contents

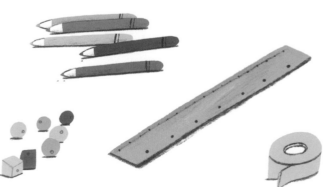

mini
MODERN ARCHITECTS

mini
CONTEMPORARY ARCHITECTS

"Architecture starts when you carefully put two bricks together. There it begins."

LUDWIG MIES VAN DER ROHE

From a very early age, children are drawn to designing spaces and making buildings. They have a strong instinct to build and are fascinated by the structures in their immediate environment. I see it in my own children every time I watch them make yet another "mini world." But what could they learn from famous historic, modern, and contemporary architecture from around the world?

The idea behind this book is to present famous buildings–from the pyramids of ancient Egypt to Zaha Hadid's contemporary, curved creations–as a starting point for mini architects to pick up concepts and explore different styles, techniques, and materials. Or, in other words, to borrow ideas from great architects and play with them!

Each of the twenty projects in this book offers an opportunity for children to learn about a renowned building or space, think about what makes it special, and then make their own mini model by following easy step-by-step instructions. I've tried and tested every activity with my children and made sure the materials are easy to come by. Many can even be recycled from household items.

This book is for all budding architects as they explore how to build the world they want to live in. Ready, set, build!

Joséphine Sebbar

Le Corbusier, impression of *Modulor Man*, cast in concrete, Nantes, France, 1955

How to use this book

Build a craft box

Each project lists the items you will need, but it can be helpful to have extra materials on hand for when you're feeling creative. Build a craft box with the essentials: white and colorful paper, pencils and pens, wushable paints, modeling clay, glue, and scissors. Collect recycled materials such as cardboard boxes and tubes, and natural objects like twigs and pebbles.

Pick the right project

Each project is unique and uses different techniques, so it's worth choosing one that suits your mini architect's mood! Keep in mind their interests and what they've been learning recently, as well as what materials you have on hand. Some projects are as simple and minimal as the buildings that inspired them, others are busy and colorful. There is something for everyone!

Discover different techniques

There are many ways to construct a building. Work with your mini architect to explore various techniques and remember to experiment. Testing out structures can be fun and rewarding, especially stacking things on top of each other! Why stop at piling up cardboard boxes? Try pebbles, paper triangles, lollipop sticks and more!

Make it your own

This book is a time machine full of buildings from around the world to inspire your mini architect. But there's no need to copy the projects exactly. The instructions are a starting point to get your own ideas flowing. Don't be afraid to mix things up. Why not create a sustainable medieval castle? What would a Zen playground look like? The architectural world is your oyster!

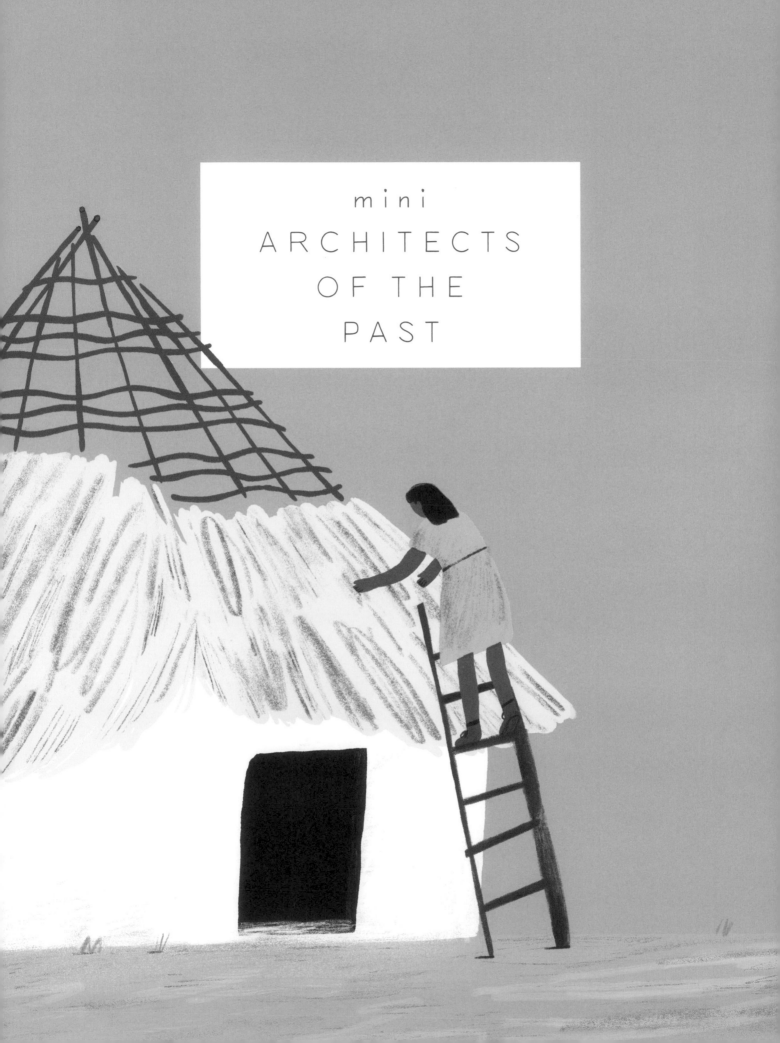

mini
ARCHITECTS
OF THE
PAST

The first architects made buildings to protect themselves from the elements and from danger. Small but perfectly formed homes such as igloos and tipis were quick to build–perfect for nomads on the move–while medieval castles took much longer to construct but offered greater protection.

Architects of the past were not only concerned with safety and shelter. Sacred spaces were important too. Some ancient structures, like the Great Pyramids of Giza and Stonehenge, are so old that archaeologists aren't sure exactly what construction methods were used. Maybe you could try to figure it out!

The projects in this section will help mini architects learn about weight, balance, and how to stack things. They will also explore simple architectural shapes such as triangles, circles, rectangles, and straight and curvy lines. You will work with stones, twigs, paper, straws, sand, and, of course, plenty of cardboard!

Ring of stones

Stonehenge

 Look at this!

Stonehenge, Wiltshire, England, c. 1800-1500 BCE

Stonehenge is a famous prehistoric monument and one of the world's biggest mysteries. It is a vast, human-made circle of enormous standing stones that was built thousands of years ago in England. It is so old that very little is known about how it was built or why.

Discuss this!

No one knows for certain how such enormous stones were transported. Some of them weighed over twenty-eight tons. That's as heavy as four elephants!

• Remember, there were no trucks or big machines to help back then! How do you think it was done?

• Can you spot the stone arches in the outer circle? How did people lift those heavy stones on top?

• What do you think Stonehenge was used for? Some of the stones line up perfectly with the sun on the shortest and longest days of the year. Could that be a clue?

 Give it a try!

Make a mini Stonehenge
out of pebbles.

you will need:

- Pebbles of various sizes
- A piece of cardboard
- Green paint
- Paint cup
- Paintbrush
- Sticky tack

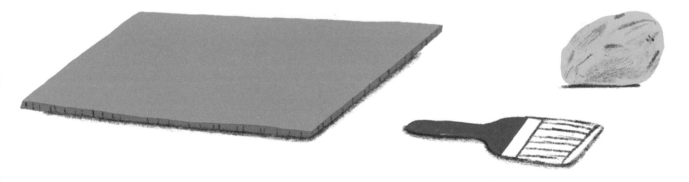

1

Collect pebbles and order them by size and shape.

2

Paint the cardboard green and let it dry. This will be your grassy base.

3

Stick little balls of sticky tack (the size of a small marble) onto the bottom of the pebbles you want to stand up.

4

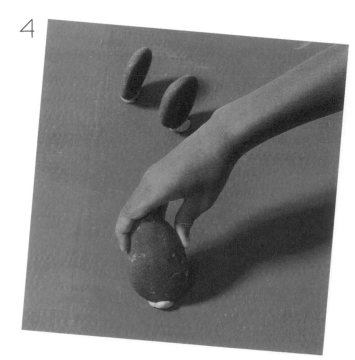

Press your pebbles down onto the cardboard base so that they stand upright. Arrange them to form a stone circle.

Tip! Pick standing stones of similar heights for your arches and position them close enough together to lay a stone on top.

5

Create a few arches by balancing pebbles across the top of two standing stones.

Try this!

What kind of games do you think the people who built Stonehenge would have played? We can't be sure! But one thing is certain: stones make great dominoes. With your leftover pebbles, why not paint a line down the middle of each one and add dots on either side to create your own stone dominoes set?

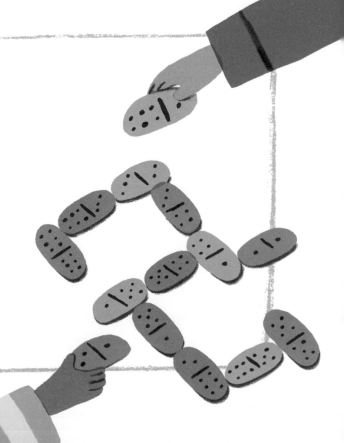

Paper pyramids

The Pyramids of Giza

 Look at this!

The Pyramids of Giza, Egypt, c. 2575-2465 BCE

The Pyramids of Giza are among the oldest and most famous monuments in the world. They were burial tombs for ancient Egyptian kings, called pharaohs. But how they were built 5,000 years ago is still a bit of a mystery. Egyptologists now think the heavy stone building blocks were dragged into place on wooden sleds.

Discuss this!

The Great Pyramid in the center is 450 feet tall. That's about the height of thirty-two double-decker buses stacked on top of each other!

• Can you imagine how far you could see if you were sitting on top of the Great Pyramid?

• The pyramids are guarded by a giant statue of a mythical creature called a sphinx. It has the head of a human and the body of a lion. What mythical creature would you choose as a bodyguard?

• Did you know that these pyramids were originally covered with white limestone and topped with a golden capstone? They would have really shined in the bright sunlight!

Give it a try!

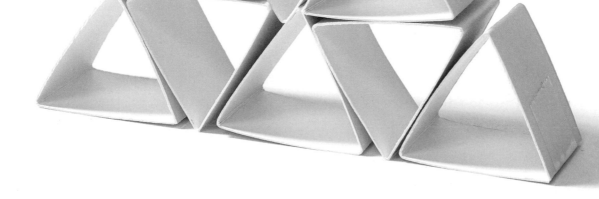

Make your own pyramid out of mini 3D triangles.

You will need:

- Thick white paper
- Thick gold paper
- Ruler
- Pencil
- Scissors
- Tape

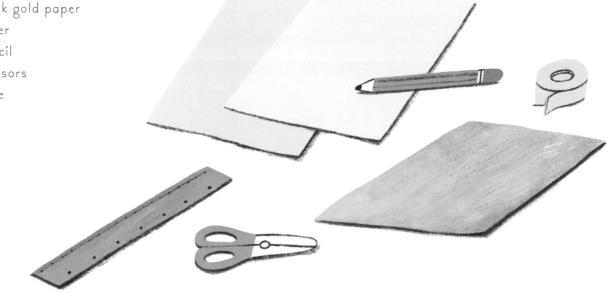

1

Use a ruler and pencil to measure out nine strips of paper, 1 x 3 inches each (eight white, one gold). Cut them out.

2

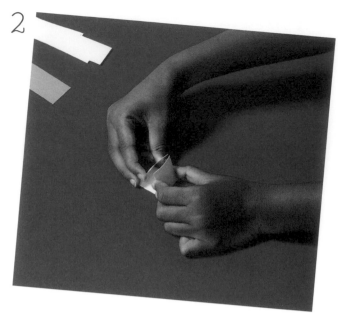

For each strip, measure 1 inch in from each end and fold to make a triangle shape.

3

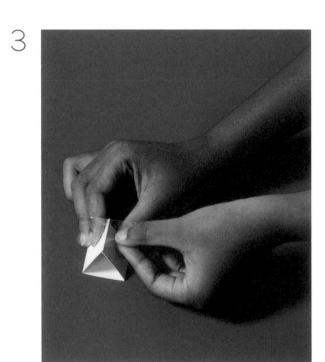

Use a small piece of tape to attach the two ends together. Repeat for each strip until you have nine triangular blocks.

4

Now it's time to build with the blocks! First, position three white triangles in a row.

Tip! If your architects are very mini, you may want to cut out and fold your paper strips ahead of time!

5

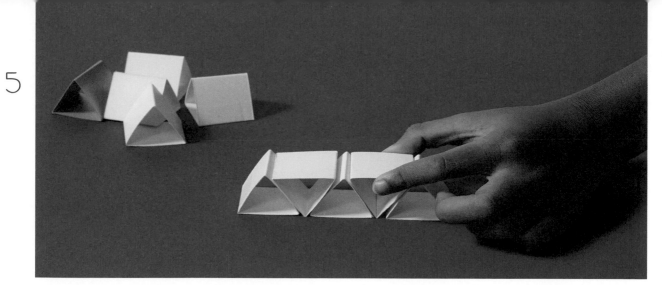

Place two more triangles facing down in between the row of three.

6

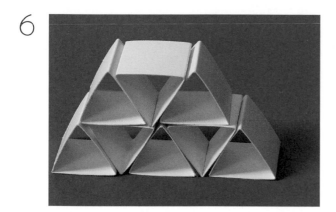

Stack two more triangles on top of your first layer and one upside down one in between.

7

Finally, place your gold triangle on top as the golden capstone.

Try this!

The Egyptians weren't the only ones to make pyramids! Build your own mini Maya-style pyramid. All you need are 55 sugar cubes. Make a square base of 5 x 5 cubes. For the next layer, center a square of 4 x 4 on top of the base. For the third layer, use 3 x 3, then 2 x 2, and finally add the last sugar cube on top!

Marble maze

The Labyrinth of Theseus

Look at this!

Theseus Mosaic from a Roman villa, Austria, c. 300 CE

This amazing pattern once covered the floor of a Roman villa. Is it a rug? No, it's a mosaic made of tiny pieces of colorful stones. It shows the labyrinth, a legendary maze from Greek mythology. Can you imagine getting lost in it? Or worse still, meeting a monster in there?

Discuss this!

Can you see the hero at the center? His name is Theseus and he has just killed the Minotaur, a fierce monster who was half-man and half-bull.

• Can you spot the entrance to the labyrinth? What about the exit?

• Who do you think was kept prisoner in the maze? Theseus or the Minotaur?

• What could a maze be built from? Walls? Hedges? What else?

 Give it a try!

Make your own maze to get lost in.
Can you get a marble to
the exit?

You will need:

- The lid of a shoebox
- Paint
- Paint cup
- Paintbrush
- Paper straws (cut to different lengths)
- Scissors
- Wooden beads (optional)
- A marble
- Craft glue
- Glue spreader or brush
- Glue cup

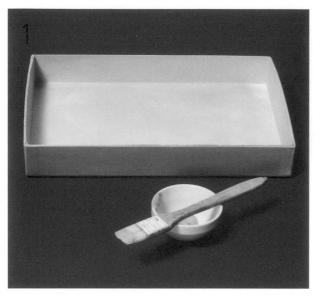

1

Paint the box lid a color of your choice and leave to dry.

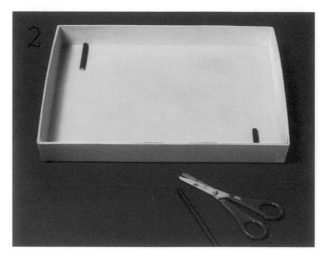

2

Place a short piece of straw at the top left corner of your box lid to mark the maze's entrance. Place another piece at the bottom right to mark the exit.

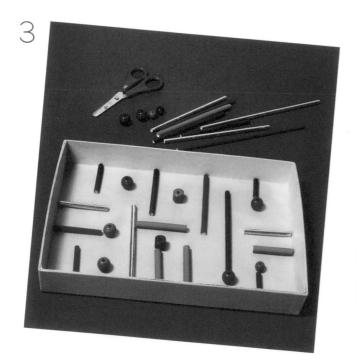

3

Place more pieces of straw in the lid and try out different path arrangements. Use wooden beads to block paths or to make the maze more challenging.

4

Test your maze with a marble to make sure it can roll along the paths you've made. Change the positions of the straws if needed.

Tip! Start by making an easy maze that has fewer elements, then challenge yourself by making it more complex.

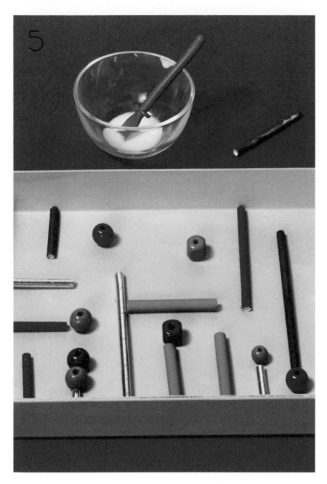

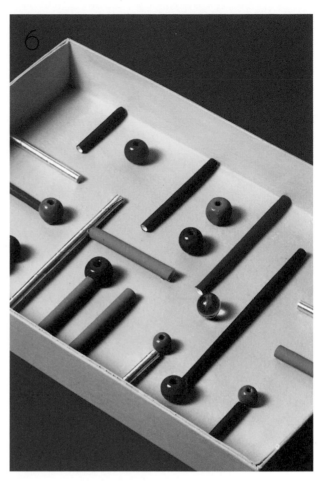

Once you're happy with your maze design, use craft glue to secure the straws and beads in place.

Once the glue is dry, you're ready to play!

Try this!

Why not make a maze out of modeling clay? Take a small chunk of modeling clay and roll it into a snake shape. Repeat until you've made at least twelve to fifteen snakes of various sizes and colors. Then make some small balls. Arrange the snakes and balls inside the cardboard box lid and press them down gently so that they stick in place. Ta-da! Another maze to play with!

Glowing igloo
Traditional Inuit dwelling

 Look at this!

Traditional Inuit igloo, North America

Not all houses have straight walls! Look at this domed home made of blocks of compacted snow. It's called an igloo. Igloos are the traditional shelters of the Inuit people of Canada's Central Arctic and the Qaanaaq area of Greenland. Today, they are sometimes still used as temporary shelters in winter.

Discuss this!

The walls of an igloo curve inward to form a dome. Look how the walls become the roof!

• Can you think of any other dome-shaped buildings? What about a planetarium?

• The light inside makes it glow. Does it look cozy?

• It can be surprisingly warm inside an igloo. The thick snow helps keep freezing cold wind out and holds body heat in. Amazing!

• An igloo is usually a single room but sometimes several are connected by tunnels to house more people. Who would you like to share an igloo with?

Give it a try!

Make a glowing
igloo out of
translucent paper.

you will need:

- Tracing paper (three sheets of 8.5 x 11 inches)
- Scissors
- Balloon
- Round bowl (a cereal bowl is perfect)
- Tape
- Marker
- Craft glue
- Water
- Glue cup
- Sponge brush
- Small glass jar
- Plastic wrap
- LED tealight

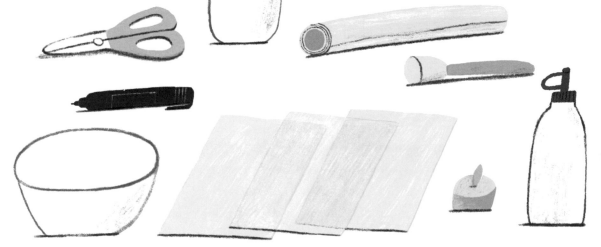

1

Cut the sheets of tracing paper
roughly into strips.

2

Blow up the balloon and place it in your
bowl. Tape it to the sides to hold it steady.
Draw a line around the middle with a
marker to indicate the igloo's base.

3

Mix water and craft glue together in a
bowl to create a papier-mâché mixture.
Use a sponge brush to spread a thin layer
of the papier-mâché mixture onto strips
of tracing paper and then stick them to
the balloon.

4

Continue to paste the strips of paper onto
the balloon until it is completely covered up
to the marked line. Then do a second layer.
This may take you some time but be patient!

Tip! Don't put too much papier-mâché mixture on the strips or they will crinkle up.
Try to stick to a maximum of two layers to allow for a quicker drying time.

5

Cover a glass jar with plastic wrap. Use more papier-mâché mixture to stick a few strips of tracing paper across the jar to make an archway shape. Leave this and the balloon to dry fully (preferably overnight).

6

Once dry, slowly deflate the balloon to leave behind your paper igloo and carefully remove your archway from the jar. Clean up any rough edges with a pair of scissors.

7

Finally, stick the archway to the igloo using tape. Then cut out a doorway underneath the archway . Put an LED tealight under the igloo to make it glow at nighttime.

Try this!

Make a nice backdrop for your igloo with some coffee filter snowflakes. Start by painting circular coffee filters with watercolor paints. Once they are dry, fold each one in half three times so they look like triangles. Cut out little slits and triangles along each side. Gently open them to reveal your snowflake designs!

Tipi hideaway

Traditional Blackfoot dwelling

 Look at this!

This special tent is called a tipi (pronounced "teepee"). It was the traditional home of the Indigenous peoples of the Great Plains of North America. Can you see the long poles sticking out at the top? These make the frame of the tipi, which was then covered in tanned buffalo skin (or later, canvas), turning it into a house in less than thirty minutes.

Blackfoot tipi, Buffalo Lodge on Little Badger, Montana, USA, 1936

Discuss this!

Some Indigenous peoples, such as the Blackfeet and Kiowa, painted their tipis with beautiful designs. Each design had a special story or meaning.

• The patterns at the bottom and top would usually represent the earth and sky. What shape would you use to show a mountain?

• The middle section would often show wild animals. What's your favorite animal to draw?

• Tipis were positioned so the entrance flap would face the rising sun. Do you know which direction your front door faces?

Give it a try!

Make your own mini tipi out of brown paper and sticks.

You will need:

- Brown paper (a paper grocery bag works well)
- Scissors
- Oil pastels or crayons
- Glue stick
- 3 sticks (around 6 inches long)
- Rubber band
- Tape
- Red paper tissue and little stones (optional)

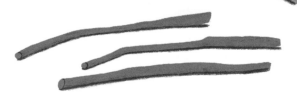

1

With the help of an adult, cut out a semicircle (roughly 8 inches in diameter) from brown paper. This will be your buffalo skin. Then cut a small semicircle in the center of the straight edge.

2

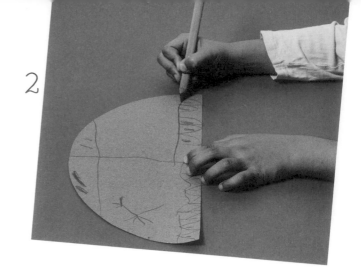

Use oil pastels or crayons to decorate the paper. Draw repeating patterns around the bottom to represent the earth, and symbols at the top for the sun, moon, or stars in the sky.

3

For the middle section, draw animals that you would find on the Great Plains, such as eagles, bison, or coyotes.

4

Shape the semicircle into a cone shape by gluing the sides together with a glue stick.

Bonus step! Make a mini firepit. Form a circle with little stones and add red tissue paper in the middle for the fire.

5

Use scissors to cut a slit for the entrance and fold the edges back into flaps.

6

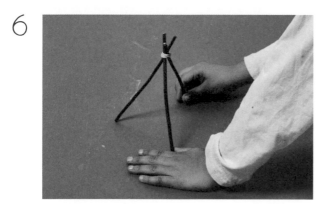

Pick three sticks and tie them together at one end with a rubber band.

7

Place the sticks inside the paper cone, with the rubber band end at the top. Spread out the sticks and tape the bottom end of each one onto the inside wall of the tipi.

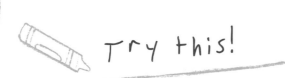

Try this!

Living in a tipi, you would always be surrounded by nature. Why not try making your own nature hideout in the woods? Start by finding a tree with a low branch forking out from the trunk. Then collect long branches and prop them so they fan out from the fork in the tree in a tipi shape. Layer more sticks on top to create a shelter, leaving room to get inside. To make it more like a tipi, you could bring along an old bedsheet to wrap around it.

Medieval fortress

Castle of Almourol

 Look at this!

Castle of Almourol, Portugal, c. 1100 CE

With its stone towers and battlements, the Castle of Almourol is a picture-perfect example of a medieval castle. Sitting on a small rocky island in the middle of the Tagus River in Portugal, it's no surprise it was used by the Knights Templar as their stronghold.

Discuss this!

Most of the castle that stands today was built in the 12th century, but parts have been rebuilt over the years. However, some foundations have been discovered that date back as far as Roman times!

- Why would building a castle on a hill surrounded by water have been a good idea?

- The little windows in the walls are called arrow slits. What do you think they were for?

- Can you think of other buildings that have been used by different people throughout history?

Give it a try!

Make your own medieval castle out of recycled cardboard and paper towel roll tubes.

You will need:

- 2 paper towel roll tubes
- Scissors
- Brown colored pencil
- Cardboard box (with sides a bit shorter than the length of a paper towel roll tube)
- Craft glue
- Glue cup
- Glue brush
- Extra cardboard or boxes
- Blue paper

1

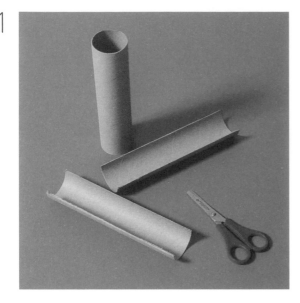

Cut both paper towel roll tubes in half to create four towers for the corners of your castle.

2

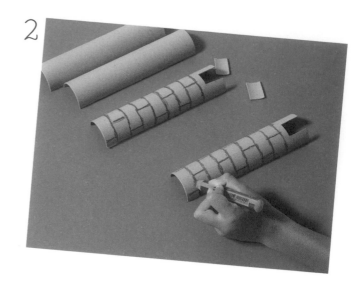

Draw a brick pattern on the four towers with a brown colored pencil and cut out little squares at the top to create the battlements.

3

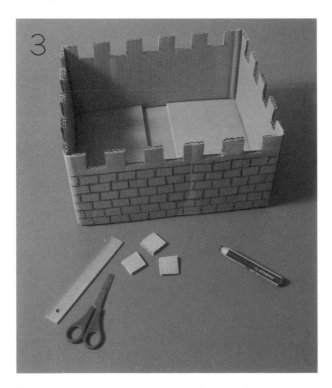

Repeat the previous step on the outside of your box. Cut out battlements at regular intervals across the top of all four sides.

4

Draw a large doorway on the front of your box and ask an adult to help cut around it.

Tip!   Don't cut across the bottom of the doorway. Leave the flap attached to act as a drawbridge!

5

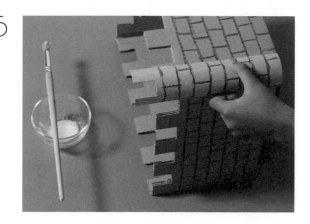

Glue a paper towel roll tower to each corner of the box.

6

Ask an adult to help you cut very narrow windows (called arrow slits) in the walls of the box.

7

Get creative and make the castle your own by adding extra details, such as more towers, balconies, and ladders, using spare cardboard and boxes. Make a moat out of blue paper and place your castle on top of it to defend it from invaders!

Try this!

Become a knight by making your own medieval shield. Draw a shield shape onto a piece of cardboard and cut it out. Draw a design for your coat of arms at the center of the shield. Animals work well! Paint it in your chosen colors and add a pattern or border to the background if you wish. Once it has dried, make a handle by taping the ends of a bent strip of cardboard to the back of your shield.

Zen garden

Ryōan-ji dry landscape garden

 Look at this!

The Kare-sansui (dry landscape) Zen garden at Ryōan-ji Temple, Kyoto, Japan, late 1400s

Gardens aren't all about trees, flowers, and plants! In this Zen temple garden in Kyoto in Japan, large rocks are arranged among white gravel. Monks carefully rake the gravel every day to help them with meditation and focus. The only greenery in the garden is some moss around the stones.

Discuss this!

Nobody knows exactly why the rocks have been placed where they are. Some people have said they look like islands in an ocean, or the peaks of mountains. Others think they represent a family of tigers crossing a river. What can you see?

• Look at the smooth patterns that have been raked into the gravel. Do they remind you of anything?

• Meditation is a way of calming your mind and body. What helps you to feel calm? A particular color, perhaps? Or the sound of running water?

• Do you like collecting pebbles from rivers or the beach?

Give it a try!

Create a mini Japanese Zen garden to meditate next to.

you will need:

- A small wooden tray or dish
- Sand
- Small stones or pebbles
  (go hunting for these outside)
- A fork (to use as a rake)
- Greenery, such as twigs or moss (optional)

1

Scoop a shallow layer of sand onto your tray or dish.

2

Smooth the surface with you hands.

3

Position your stones in the sand. You can choose to form a path or place them randomly. Just pick the spots that feel right to you.

4

You could choose to add in extra features, like moss around the stones. Twigs and leaves can be used to make trees.

Tip! Zen gardens are peaceful places, so we recommend drawing curves and circles in the sand as these shapes are well known for bringing calm.

5

Then use your fork to rake the sand. Enjoy drawing different patterns. Try making ripples around the stones.

Try this!

In Japan, Torii gates are often used to mark the entrance of sacred spaces, such as Shinto shrines and occasionally Buddhist temples. They are painted in vermilion, a bright red color that represents wisdom in Japanese culture. Make a mini version by gluing popsicle sticks together and painting them red. Place your gate into the sand at the entrance of your Zen garden.

mini
MODERN
ARCHITECTS

At the end of the 19th century, the use of iron and steel and advancements in machinery allowed architects and engineers, such as Antoni Gaudí and Gustave Eiffel, to build stronger, taller, and lighter buildings than ever before. The results include some of the world's most iconic buildings, like the Sagrada Família in Barcelona, and the Eiffel Tower in Paris. Around the same time, the first skyscrapers appeared in the U.S. In the 20th century, modern architects celebrated buildings that were practical and free of decoration—a style we now call "minimalism." Modern architects like Le Corbusier created geometric buildings from reinforced concrete, while Charles and Ray Eames used large glass panels to make their house light and see-through. It's not just mini architects that experiment with new materials! So, free your inner modern architect and make a temple inspired by Gaudí, a mini Eiffel tower, your own version of the Manhattan skyline, a dream modular house, a Brutalist block of apartments, a floating opera house . . . and even a monster playground!

Spaghetti temple

Sagrada Família

 Look at this!

It's no surprise that three million people visit the Sagrada Família in Barcelona every year. It was designed by Antoni Gaudí and is one of the most ambitious and talked about architectural projects ever! The cathedral has eighteen towers and is covered in lots of detailed carvings, which have a lot of meaning and stories behind them.

Antoni Gaudí, *Sagrada Família*, Barcelona, Spain, 1882-2026

Discuss this!

Construction of the Sagrada Família started over 140 years ago, in 1882, and it's not planned to be completed until 2026!

• What's the longest project you've ever worked on?

• Can you tell that Gaudí was inspired by nature? The pillars inside even look like trees!

• At the beginning of its construction, a school was built in the cathedral for the children of the builders to go to. Would you like to go to school in a building like this?

Give it a try!

Create a fancy tower, inspired by the Sagrada Família, using spaghetti and marshmallows.

You will need:

- 11 regular marshmallows
- 7 mini marshmallows
- 10 pieces of dry spaghetti
  (we recommend having extra
  on hand in case you break any)

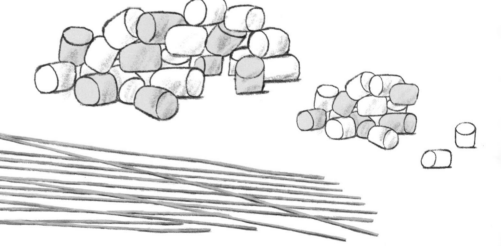

1

Break three pieces of spaghetti into quarters, so you have twelve equal pieces. Use six of these pieces to join six marshmallows together in a circle.

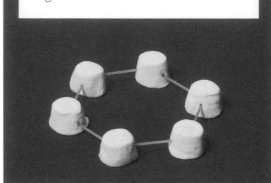

2

Place a marshmallow in the center of the circle and connect it to each of the outer marshmallows using the remaining short pieces of spaghetti.

3

Put half a stick of spaghetti upright into each of the outer marshmallows. Then stick three more into the central marshmallow, positioning them in between the spokes of the circle.

4

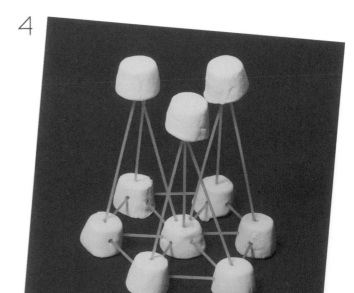

Pull one piece of spaghetti from the middle marshmallow and two of the outer pieces together into a pyramid shape and top with a marshmallow. Repeat twice more so there are three pyramids.

Tip! Push the spaghetti far enough into the marshmallows so that it feels stable, but not far enough to come through the opposite side.

5

Stick half a piece of spaghetti into
the top of the three marshmallows added
in the previous step and pull the ends
together into a point. Then top with
a final marshmallow.

6

Break seven short pieces of spaghetti and
stick them into the top marshmallow
in a star shape. Top each piece with
a mini marshmallow.

Try this!

Make some brightly colorful towers using
leftover spaghetti and some colorful straws.
Stand your lengths of spaghetti upright
in some modeling clay to hold them
steady, then cut your straws into short
pieces and thread as many as you can
onto the spaghetti.

Tower of straws

Eiffel Tower

Look at this!

Gustave Eiffel, *The Eiffel Tower*, Paris, France, 1889

Do you recognize this building? The Eiffel Tower in Paris is one of the most famous buildings in the world. Built in 1889, it was meant to be temporary but it was allowed to stay, partly because it was a good place to put a radio transmitter! Steel is much stronger than stone or bricks but it also rusts when it gets wet. The whole tower needs to be repainted every seven years. That's quite a job!

Discuss this!

The Eiffel Tower is almost a thousand feet tall. That's about as tall as thirty elephants stacked on top of each other!

• Do you think you could climb to the top in less than an hour? How long would you need to climb the 1,665 steps? Or would you rather take the elevator?

• Towers make a wonderful lookout. What could you see if you built a tower in your neighborhood?

• Can you name another tall building made of metal? How about other things? Railroad tracks?

Give it a try!

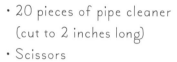

Make your own mini
Eiffel Tower out of straws.

You will need:

- 15 paper straws
- Paint
- Paint cup
- Paintbrush
- 20 pieces of pipe cleaner
  (cut to 2 inches long)
- Scissors
- Washi tape

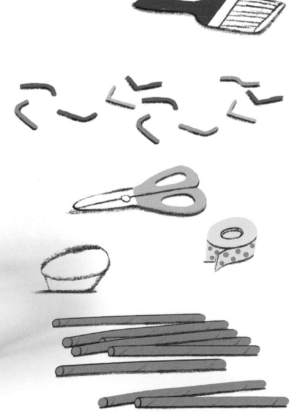

1

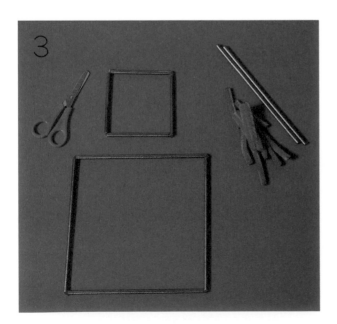

Paint the straws in the color of your choice and leave to dry.

2

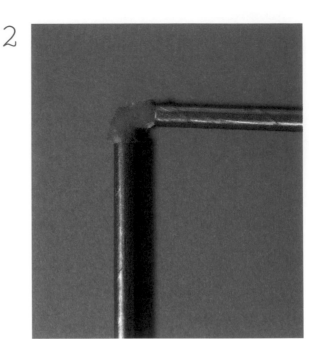

Join two straws by bending a piece of pipe cleaner into a right angle and inserting the ends into each straw.

3

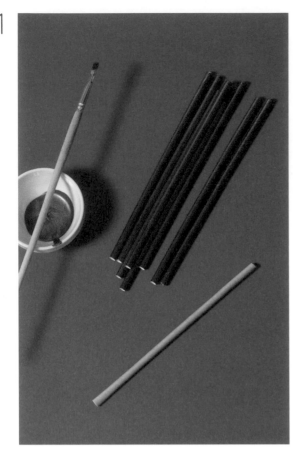

Repeat the previous step to make a square of straws, joined at the corners with pipe cleaners. Then cut two more straws in half and make a smaller square the same way.

4

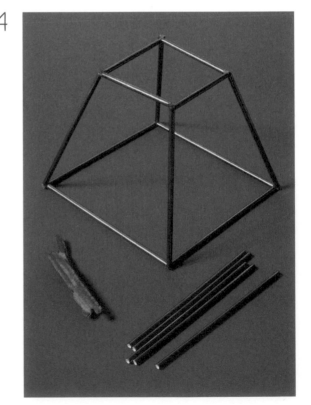

Use four more straws to connect the two squares together at the corners. Connect each joint with another piece of pipe cleaner.

5

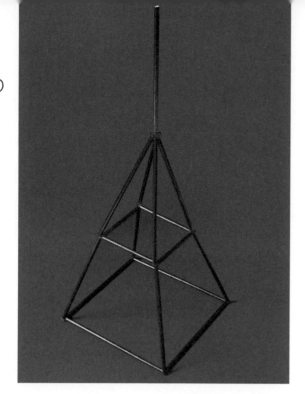

Add another four straws to the corners
of the smaller square. Use pipe cleaner
pieces to join the ends together into a point
and add a final straw on top. This is your
radio transmitter!

6

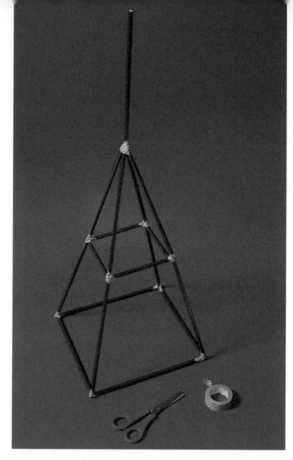

Secure all your joints with washi tape.

Tip! Wrapping washi tape around all of the joints will make your
tower extra strong and stable.

Try this!

Next time, why not build a tower
out of cubes? Make two cubes and
stack them on top of each other.
Repeat and see how high you can
go. You might be able to build the
highest straw tower in the world!
Why not try other shapes for your
base, such as a hexagon (six sides),
or an octagon (eight sides)?

Giant skyscrapers

New York skyline

Look at this!

View of Manhattan, New York, USA

New York is famous for its skyscrapers. The city is home to more than 7,000 buildings that are at least 114 feet high (and three hundred that are 490 feet or more!). These can mostly be found in the busy borough of Manhattan.

Discuss this!

One of the perks of high-rise living is being at the heart of everything–close to school, public transit, and the fun of the city–not to mention the view!

• Can you spot the Hudson River? What about the iconic Empire State Building?

• Can you believe that the oldest skyscrapers are more than 100 years old already? Don't they look modern?

• What would be the best thing about living on the 50th floor of a skyscraper? Can you picture the view from your bedroom?

Give it a try!

Create your own mini Manhattan with boxes!

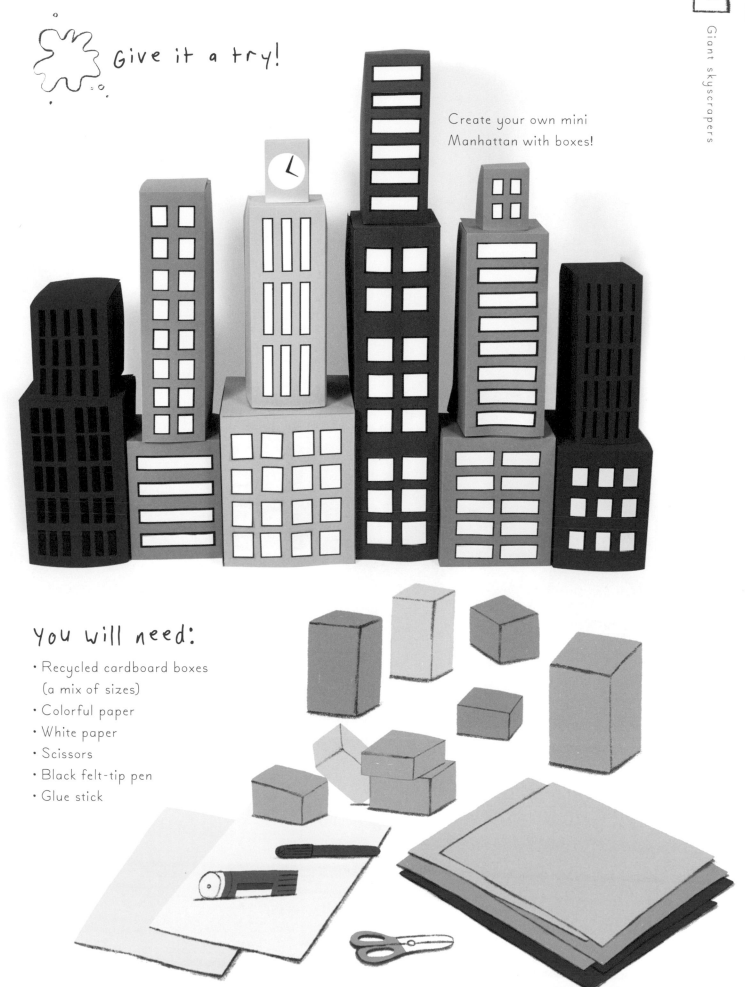

You will need:

- Recycled cardboard boxes (a mix of sizes)
- Colorful paper
- White paper
- Scissors
- Black felt-tip pen
- Glue stick

1

Gather as many cardboard boxes of various sizes as you can! We recommend a minimum of twelve. Experiment by stacking your boxes to create multiple skyscraper towers.

2

Cut colorful paper to size to cover the sides of each box and glue in place. Use one color for each skyscraper.

3

Cut out paper rectangles to use as windows. You might want to cut different sizes and shapes for different buildings.

4

Use a black felt-tip pen to draw around the edges of your windows. These are your window frames!

Tip! Use a black felt-tip pen to add extra details. Why not try drawing some balconies, or a clock tower?

5

Arrange the windows on your
buildings in a grid and glue them
in place. You could also leave some
buildings without windows.

6

Stack the skyscrapers and arrange them
into your own skyline.

Try this!

Why not make a pop-up skyline card? First,
fold a piece of thick paper or card stock in half.
Then cut three pairs of slits along the folded
edge to create three tabs. You can make the tabs
different lengths and widths. Open the card
and fold the cut tabs inward so that they pop
up into three skyscrapers. Draw details on the
buildings and the neighborhood around them.

Building cards

The Eames House

 Look at this!

Charles and Ray Eames, *The Eames House*, Santa Monica, USA, 1949

Charles and Ray Eames designed and built this house in California in 1949 to live and work in. It was designed using ready-made blocks arranged in a modular grid. "Modular" means that each piece has the same basic shape and different elements can be added and moved around. This way of building is easy and not too expensive.

Discuss this!

Look at the outside of the house. It's a steel grid, filled with glass windows and panels of different colors. It looks sort of like a huge Rubik's Cube.

• Imagine a house that could be changed to suit what you like to do. How would you change your own house to make it more of a reading house? Or a sleeping house? Or a playing house?

• What would your dream house look like?

• Would you like to be able to take off the roof of your house on a sunny day?

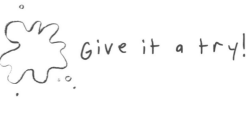

Give it a try!

Make your own set of
building cards and use it
to build your dream house.

You will need:

- Strong cardboard
- Ruler
- Pencil
- Scissors
- Paint (acrylic paint is best)
- Paint cups
- Paintbrushes

1

Cut out around thirty cardboard squares and rectangles. These will become your building cards. Cards with 2 inch sides are easiest for little hands to grasp.

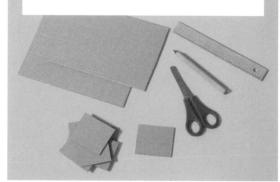

2

Cut some very narrow V-shaped slits along the edges, or at the corners, of each card. Each slit should be about half an inch long.

3

Paint your cards the same colors as the Eames House: black, white, red, yellow, and blue. Use acrylic paint if you can as it will make the cardboard tougher and less likely to rip. Let the paint dry completely.

4

Slot one card into another. Keep building until you've made your dream house. Re-design and re-build to your heart's content.

Tip! The slits should never extend more than halfway through each cardboard shape.

5

Now that you have your own building card set, the options are endless! Why not try building a flat house, or a tall house?

Try this!

Instead of making square and rectangular cards, try creating some other shapes, such as circles, and triangles. Add simple patterns, like stripes, or dots, when you paint them.

Tower block box

Cité Radieuse

 Look at this!

Le Corbusier, *Cité Radieuse*, Marseille, France, 1952

The Cité Radieuse in Marseille is the most famous of the Unité d'habitation (Housing Units), and perhaps Le Corbusier's most iconic work. The concrete tower block is comprised of 337 apartments across eighteen storeys, and has inspired many other buildings in the Brutalist style.

Discuss this!

The building has a lot of shared spaces and is very child-friendly. It even has a kiddie pool on its roof terrace and an art school for children.

• Can you see that the building is standing on large columns, like stilts? How many can you count?

• Do you think a building can help the people that live there feel happy? What makes you happy in your home?

• In your home, where is your favorite place to spend time with friends and family? Where do you go to be alone?

Give it a try!

Make a mini Brutalist tower block out of a shoebox and cardboard.

You will need:

- Cardboard box
- Thick corrugated cardboard (the chunkier the better)
- Scissors
- Masking tape
- Paint (red, blue, yellow, and white)
- Paint cups
- Paintbrushes

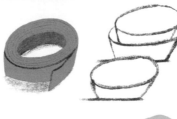

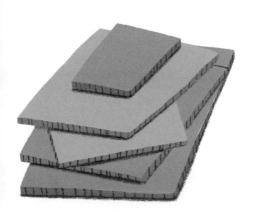

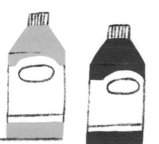

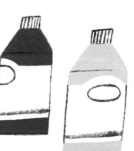

1

Cut a piece of corrugated cardboard to fit snugly across the length of your box to make two floors.

2

Cut two more cardboard pieces to fit across the width, on either side of the first piece. Assemble to create four apartments in your tower block. Secure the cardboard in place with masking tape if needed.

3

Paint the inside of each apartment in a different color. Use red, yellow, blue, and white to make it look like the Cité Radieuse.

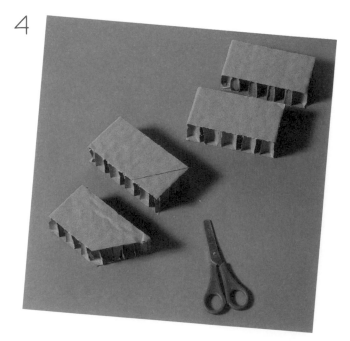

4

Cut out four identical cardboard rectangles to create the columns for your tower block to stand on. Cut a thin triangle from one short side of each rectangle to turn them into trapezoid shapes.

With the shortest edge of each column at the bottom and the slanted side facing the front, evenly space your columns along the base of your tower block and attach them with masking tape.

Turn your tower block the right way up. Do you have any toys that might like to live inside the apartments? You could even try making some cardboard furniture to decorate them!

Tip! Make sure your columns are thick enough to support the weight of the structure. You could make extras and stick them together if necessary.

Try this!

The Cité Radieuse is surrounded by trees in the center of a large park. Why not make trees out of leftover cardboard to put around your block of apartments? Feel free to add other details as well, such as a kiddie pool on the rooftop!

Monster park

The Golem

 Look at this!

Niki de Saint Phalle, *The Golem*, Rabinovich Park, West Jerusalem, Israel, 1972

Look how many tongues this black and white monster has! Can you believe those tongues are used as slides? This creature is called The Golem and it is part of artist Niki de Saint Phalle's architectural playground for the Rabinovich Park in West Jerusalem.

Discuss this!

The design for The Golem was initially rejected for being too scary, but Saint Phalle's answer was that "scary things are good because they help children conquer their fears."

• Do you find the monster scary, or could it be friendly?

• On its opening day, there was a big party with balloons, flags, and many children playing on the slides. Have you ever been to a party in a park?

• The artist enjoyed designing this play structure so much that she went on to create a sculpture garden park. What would you include in your dream playground?

Give it a try!

Design your dream
playground, including
a friendly monster
with tongue
slides.

You will need:

- Shoebox lid
- Scrap paper
- Modeling clay
- Jumbo craft stick
- Drinking straw
- Beads
- Craft glue
- Pipe cleaners

1

Using the lid of a shoebox as the base for your playground, start by making your monster as a centerpiece! First, scrunch up a piece of scrap paper into roughly the shape you want its body to be.

2

Flatten out a piece of modeling clay to cover the paper. Continue to mold it and add extra pieces of clay until you're happy with your monster's body.

3

Give it a face and make three tongues out of red modeling clay to use as slides. It's your own version of The Golem!

4

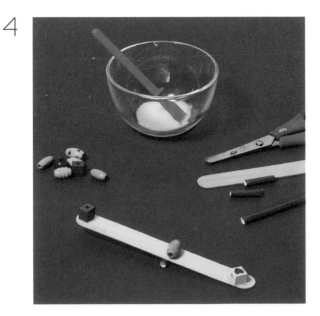

Here are some more fun ideas to add to your playground, starting with a simple seesaw. Glue a jumbo craft stick to a piece of a drinking straw. It's a sees(tr)aw! Decorate with beads.

Tip! Ask an adult to make some holes in your shoebox lid. Push the ends of your pipe cleaner structures through to keep them upright.

5

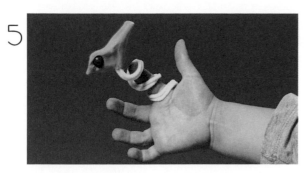

To make a spring rider, create a little animal out of modeling clay. Then wrap a pipe cleaner around your finger to make a spiral and stick the animal onto one end.

6

Make a jungle gym using pipe cleaners. Experiment by twisting them into different shapes and threading beads onto them.

7

Arrange all of your playground structures onto your shoebox lid base. But don't stop there! What else could you add? What about monkey bars or a swing?

 **Try this!**

What would a park be without a fountain? Make a water feature out of leftover pipe cleaners and other craft elements to add next to your playground. Take a small tray or dish and fill it with water. Create a sculpture or two to place in it, inspired by the Fountain Stravinsky in Paris. What will your sculptures represent? A serpent, a heart, or perhaps a mermaid? Ocean animals would work particularly well.

Floating building

Sydney Opera House

 Look at this!

Jørn Utzon, *Sydney Opera House*, Sydney, Australia, 1973

The Sydney Opera House is a very unique building that is easily recognizable, thanks to its incredible "shells" made of concrete. The building sits proudly on Sydney Harbor and looks like a boat with big sails.

Discuss this!

Take a closer look—are all the sail-shaped shells pointing in the same direction? Can you count them?

• Do you agree that the opera house looks like a sailing boat? Or does it look like something else to you?

• Would you like to go inside? The temperature in there is always a comfortable 72.5°F so that the orchestra's instruments stay in tune for performances.

• Despite its name, the venue doesn't only host operas! It has a busy program, including events for children. What show would you love to see there?

Give it a try!

Make a floating
Sydney Opera
House out of
paper plates!

You will need:

- 6 paper plates
- Pencil
- Scissors
- Stapler
- Tape
- Tin foil

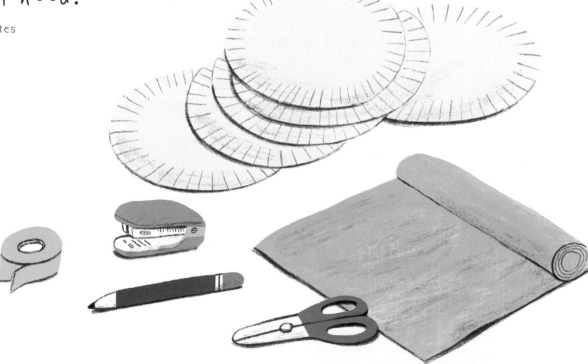

1

First, draw a thin eye shape in the middle of five of the plates.

2

Cut along your lines in order to make ten crescent shapes.

3

Pair up the crescents, with the plates facing inward. Staple about 2 inches in from the corners of each pair. You have made your five shells.

4

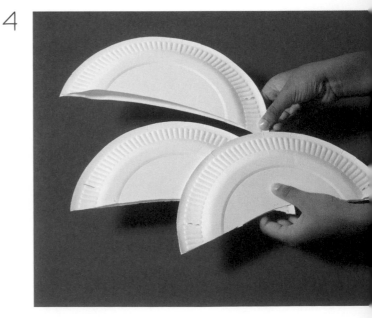

Open up the edge of one of the shells and slot the others inside, arranging them to look like the opera house. Then staple them together.

Fold over the corners of the bottom shell to create two tabs and attach them to the middle of the remaining plate with tape.

Wrap the base plate in tin foil to make it waterproof. Then try floating it on water.

Tip! A sink or bath is a good place to float your opera house. Or you could even try floating it outside on a pond!

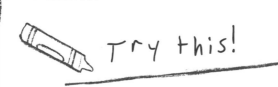 **Try this!**

Let's make cork sailing boats to go with your opera house. First, choose three recycled corks and join them together with two elastic bands to make a raft. Then, cut out a sail from colorful paper and thread it onto a toothpick. Stick your sail into the center of the raft. Now it's ready to float!

mini
CONTEMPORARY
ARCHITECTS

In the last twenty years, architects have been experimenting more than ever—exploring materials, taking inspiration from the past, and engaging with current challenges. Today, it's less about building higher and more about experimenting, and testing the rules of architecture. In this section, mini architects will be introduced to the futuristic shapes of Zaha Hadid, and revisit familiar forms in a playful and colorful way with artist Tom Fruin. Importantly, we will also look at how contemporary architects are responding to the challenges of climate change in creative and inspiring ways. See how Singapore-based designers WOHA have embraced nature in their hotel overrun with plants, and how Mariam Issoufou Kamara worked with locally sourced, sustainable materials to build the Dandaji market in Niger. By exploring the various projects in this section, mini architects will discover how green technology can influence the future of architecture without losing sight of how creative designing and building can be!

Curvy constructions

Heydar Aliyev Centre

Look at this!

Zaha Hadid, *Heydar Aliyev Centre*, Baku, Azerbaijan, 2012

The Heydar Aliyev Centre in Baku looks like a big wave that is about to crash on the rocks. It is famous for its curved shapes. It was designed by Zaha Hadid, an architect known for her futuristic style, and for playing with forms to create unusual-looking buildings.

Discuss this!

The smooth shapes of the building are very striking. Your eye can easily follow its flowing curves.

• Can you follow the curving shape of the building with your finger?

• Can you imagine using the building as a giant slide?

• What things from nature does the building remind you of? A shell? The wind? What about the waves of the nearby Caspian Sea?

Give it a try!

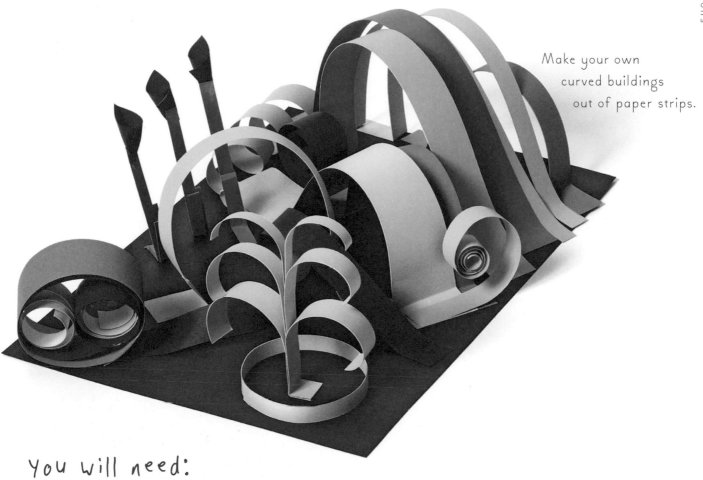

Make your own curved buildings out of paper strips.

You will need:

- Colorful paper
- Ruler
- Pencil
- Scissors
- Glue stick

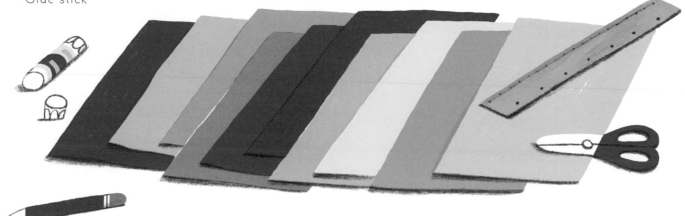

1

Use a pencil and ruler to draw straight lines across sheets of colorful paper. Cut along the lines to create strips of various lengths, widths, and colors.

2

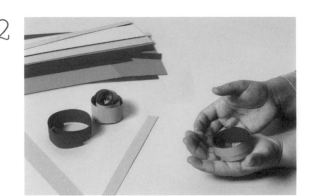

Experiment with rolling and folding the paper to create different shapes and curves. Practice making spirals and circles.

4

Start building! Apply glue to the tabs of the first strip and then press it down onto a sheet of paper. Hold it for ten seconds to secure it.

3

Fold a short tab at the end of each piece of paper so that you can stick it down later.

Tip! Younger children might prefer tearing the strips of paper rather than cutting them. This is fine as long as you don't mind a rougher effect.

5

6

Continue to add paper strips until you are happy with the overall look of your construction. Add as many loops and curves as you wish.

Add some extra details such as a fountain or some flower beds made out of paper spirals.

 Try this!

Instead of designing your building in 3D, you might prefer to plan it out flat, in 2D. Design your ideal house by arranging and gluing down whole paper strips onto a sheet of paper. Think about shapes when creating your design. Do you prefer a building that is curvy, like a circle, or angular, like a triangle?

Stained glass tower

Tom Fruin's Watertower

 Look at this!

Tom Fruin, *Watertower*, New York, USA, 2012

Look at all the different colors in this beautiful water tower. Artist Tom Fruin has reimagined the traditional wooden water tower, using different materials and colors to turn it into a work of art. The iconic sculpture that sits on the rooftop of a New York building can hold up to 10,000 gallons of water!

Discuss this!

It is made of steel and about 1,000 scraps of recycled plexiglass, which make it look like a stained glass lantern.

• What do you think lights up the tower during the night? The moon? Street lights?

• Water towers store a lot of water! Can you think of any other types of large structures that are used to store things?

• Can you name a colorful material that you wish was used in more modern buildings?

Give it a try!

Make your
own light-up
water tower.

You will need:

- Glass jar (remove any existing labels)
- Tissue paper in assorted colors
  (precut into small squares or strips)
- Craft glue
- Water
- Glue cup
- Glue brush
- Jumbo craft sticks
- Wooden clothespins
- LED tealight

1

Mix water and craft glue together in a bowl to create a papier-mâché mixture. Use a small brush to cover your jar with the papier-mâché mixture.

2

Press tissue paper squares onto the jar to cover it. Overlap the squares slightly to avoid gaps and to create new colors.

3

Wait for the jar to dry before painting an extra layer of your papier-mâché mixture over the top to secure the tissue paper and act as a varnish. Leave to dry.

4

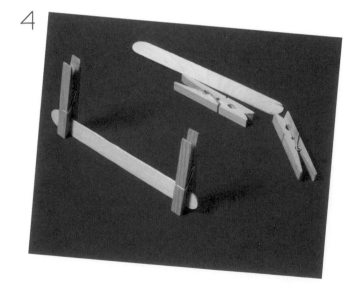

Create two supports for the stand of your water tower by clipping clothespins to each end of two jumbo craft sticks.

Tip! Having tissue paper already cut into small pieces makes this activity easier for younger children.

5

6

To learn how to make the top of the stand, turn to page 90 and follow steps one and two. Once it's dry, glue it on top of the supports.

Place your jar on top of the stand with an LED tealight inside it to create a colorful night-light.

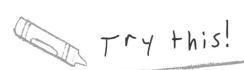

Try this!

Next, why don't you make a nature-inspired water tower by using natural materials instead of tissue paper? Collect flowers and petals in spring and fallen leaves in autumn. Use the same steps as above and don't forget the final sealing layer of papier-mâché mixture to give your water tower a rich finish.

Green city
PARKROYAL COLLECTION Pickering

Look at this!

WOHA, *PARKROYAL COLLECTION Pickering*, Singapore, 2013

This high-rise hotel is so green! It looks like it's made out of glass, trees, and plants. Celebrating Singapore's tropical ecosystem, the architects wanted to show that greenery can make a building stand out and be both attractive and sustainable. What's not to like?

Discuss this!

Do you like to be surrounded by plants-indoors as well as outdoors? How does being around plants make you feel?

• Can you imagine the view from inside this hotel? You might think you were in the jungle!

• Do you have a favorite type of plant?

• How do you think green buildings like this might also help birds and insects?

 Give it a try!

Make your own
sustainable hotel for
your favorite toys . . .
or bugs!

 You will need:

- Thick corrugated cardboard
  (the chunkier the better)
- Regular cardboard
- Scissors
- Craft glue
- Glue cup
- Glue spreader or brush
- Greenery, such as branches, leaves, and moss

1

Gather together cardboard pieces to make your hotel. You will need at least one large piece of regular cardboard for the base and two tall pieces of thick corrugated cardboard to form the walls.

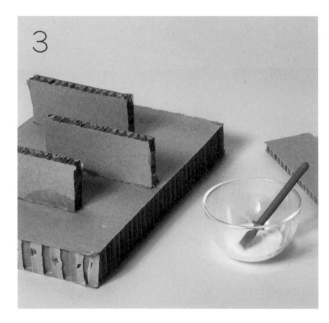

2

Cut out long, thin pieces of the corrugated cardboard to make balconies.

3

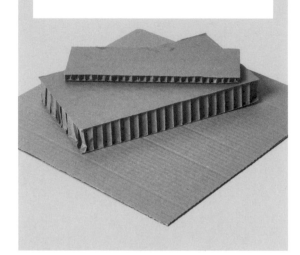

Glue the balcony pieces onto the cardboard walls.

4

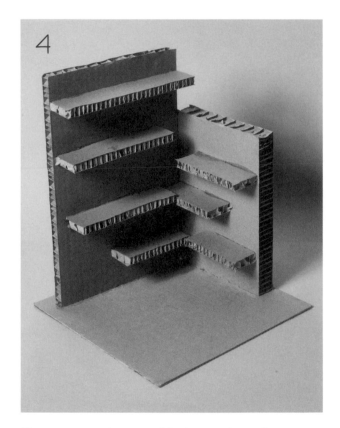

Once you are happy with the number of balconies, stand the two walls upright and stick them onto the base by applying craft glue to the bottom edges. Apply pressure for a few minutes and then leave it to dry for another five minutes.

Tip! If you don't have chunky corrugated cardboard, glue several layers of regular corrugated cardboard together instead.

5

6

Turn your building into a green oasis by sticking branches and leaves through the holes in the cardboard. You can also add more greenery by arranging leaves around the base and on the balconies.

Invite your favorite tropical animals to visit, especially bugs and birds that can fly to the higher levels.

Try this!

Make your own hanging garden from recycled plastic pots (old fruit containers are great because they already have drainage holes). Ask an adult to make holes in the top corners of each pot to thread string through. Tie the pots on top of each other, like a ladder, using long pieces of string. Fill your pot with compost and add some small plants, such as herbs. Hang your garden against a wall or in a window. Don't forget to water it!

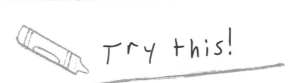

Parasol market

Dandaji market

 Look at this!

Mariam Issoufou Kamara, Atelier Masōmi, *Dandaji market*, Niger, 2018

The colorful canopies provide the sellers and visitors of this market in Niger with shelter from the heat of the sun. The fifty-two market stalls are made from compressed earth bricks and have been built around an old ancestral tree.

Discuss this!

In this rural area, the market is a central meeting place for the local community to enjoy.

• The architect, Mariam Issoufou Kamara, used recycled local metal to build the colorful circular canopies. What do they remind you of? Lily pads? Trees? Giant umbrellas?

• The canopies were built to make up for the lack of trees, which are hard to grow in such a hot, dry climate. They also look great! Which is your favorite color?

• Can you see that they are set at different heights? This helps with airflow to keep the people and produce in the market stalls cool.

Give it a try!

You will need:

- 3 metal lids (from jelly jars, or similar)
- Acrylic paint (blue, green, and yellow)
- Paintbrushes
- Paint cups
- 3 paper straws
- Rubber band
- Tape
- Air-dry clay
- Modeling tools (optional)
- Paper
- Colored pencils or crayons

Design a colorful metal canopy and market stall out of recycled jar lids and clay.

1

Thoroughly wash and dry your lids before painting each one a different color (blue, green, or yellow).

2

Make the stand for the canopy by tying the three straws together with a rubber band.

3

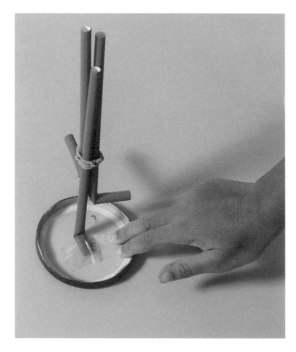

Bend over the tops of each straw and arrange them at different levels. Then attach one to the bottom of each lid with tape.

4

Build your market stall out of air-dry clay. Give it a square base and three sides, leaving it open at the front. Make a hole in one corner for your canopy to fit into.

Tip! Make the walls of your stall nice and thick so they are strong enough to support the canopy.

Insert the straws of your canopy into the corner and gently press the clay around it to secure. Add some extra clay if necessary. Leave the stall to dry fully.

Draw some fruits and vegetables to go on your stall. Bananas, pineapples, and mangoes all grow in Niger. Cut them out and arrange them in your stall to bring it to life!

Try this!

At Dandaji market you will find lots of things to buy. As well as fresh fruit and vegetables, there are stalls selling colorful, patterned clothing and fabrics. Using paper, markers, and colored pencils, design your own bold fabric patterns. Cut your patterned paper into clothing shapes, and little squares of fabric to add to your market stall.

Stacking structure

Odunpazari Modern Museum

 Look at this!

Kengo Kuma, *Odunpazari Modern Museum*, Turkey, 2019

Buildings sometimes have a strong bond with their location. That is the case for the Odunpazari Modern Museum in Turkey. Japanese architect Kengo Kuma was inspired by the historical wooden market and traditional Ottoman houses in the local area.

Discuss this!

The museum's design looks like a stack of slatted timber boxes.

• Can you see how all the boxes interlink? It looks kind of like a giant 3D jigsaw puzzle!

• Can you think of some examples of other wooden buildings?

• Do you know anything about the local history around where you live? Do lots of the buildings near you look alike?

Give it a try!

Build your own stacked wooden
structure out of craft sticks
and wooden clothespins.

you will need:

- Jumbo craft sticks
- Craft glue
- Glue cup
- Glue spreader or brush
- Wooden clothespins

1

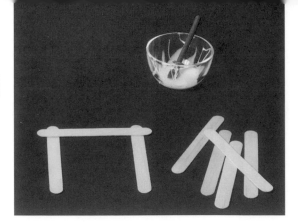

Start by making a frame out of four
jumbo craft sticks by gluing the ends
together to form a square.

2

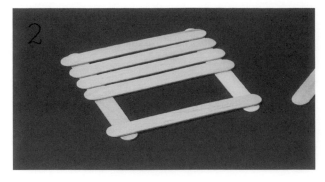

Glue more craft sticks onto the frame
in a line to create a slatted panel.

3

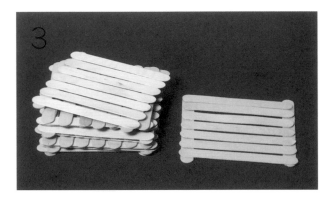

Repeat the previous steps until you have at
least eight panels. These will become the walls,
ceilings, and floors of your building.

4

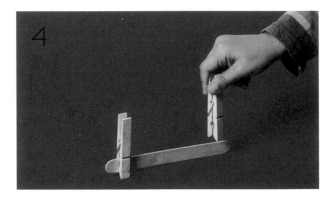

Create supports by clipping a clothespin
to each end of a craft stick. Start by making
at least ten of these.

5

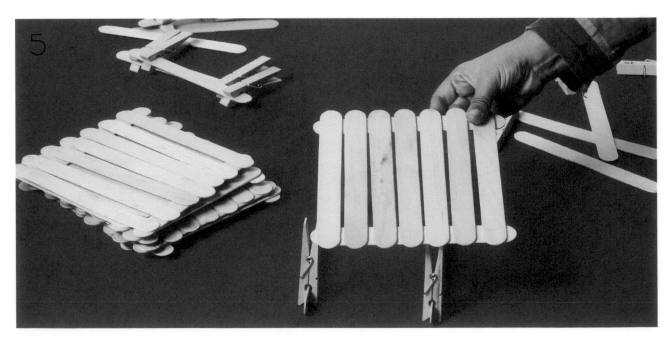

Now that you have your panels and supports, you are ready
to build! Start by balancing a panel on top of two supports.

6 Build upward by placing supports on top of your first layer and balancing panels on them. Create as many stories as you like!

7 Experiment with different layouts, building out as well as up! Give your building walls by propping more panels up against the sides of the supports.

Tip! Two clothespins with a craft stick between them make great supports for a structure. It's much more stable than clothespins on their own.

Try this!

Sometimes breaking a structure can be as much fun as building one. Why not make a rainbow domino chain? First, color in twelve craft sticks with paint or felt-tip pens. Attach two clothespins to each stick and stand them in a line, about half an inch apart. Push the last one over and watch them all topple!

Eco clay den

TECLA house

 Look at this!

MCA - Mario Cucinella Architects, *TECLA-Technology and Clay*, Italy, 2021

This is a prototype for the world's first entirely 3D-printed house made using clay from the local environment. The name *TECLA* combines "tec" from technology and "cla" from clay. This house is an eco-friendly building made using only natural, recycled, and reusable materials.

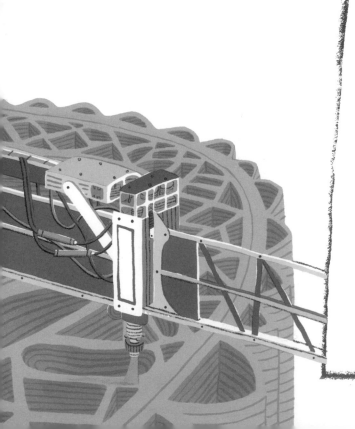

Discuss this!

Architect Mario Cucinella and 3D printing specialists WASP developed this idea as a way to make climate-friendly housing, combining ancient building materials and techniques with new technology.

• Does its domed shape remind you of anything? The design was inspired by potter wasps, who make their nests out of mud.

• Can you imagine a house coming out of a printer? Instead of paper and ink, very special printers squirt out layer after layer of clay, which slowly builds up into a house!

• Can you think of some benefits of using local and natural materials?

Give it a try!

Build a coiled
clay den.

You will need:

- Air-dry clay
- Small bowl of water
  (for wetting the clay
  and cleaning fingers)
- Modeling tool (or a table knife)

1

Roll out pieces of clay between your fingers and the work surface to create long snakes, about half an inch thick.

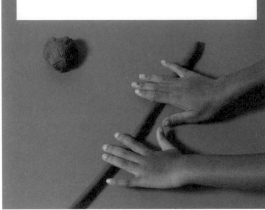

2

Make the bottom layer of your den by forming one length of clay into a circle. If it is too long, wrap one end round on top to start the next layer.

3

Join the end of your first length of clay with a new one and coil it around on top of your first circle. Push it down a bit so the layers stick together.

4

Keep adding layers in a spiral, making each circle slightly smaller than the last so it starts to form a dome.

Tip! You can also use water to smooth out the areas between your lengths of clay and help stick them together.

5

Leave a small opening as a skylight.

6

Repeat steps 1-5 to make a second mini den.

7

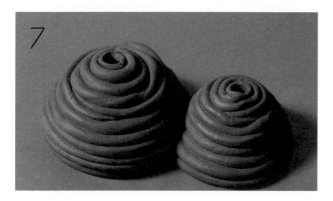

Carefully join the sides of your two dens together to form a den with two rooms, like the TECLA house.

8

Use a modeling tool or a table knife to cut a doorway. Then leave your building to dry fully.

Try this!

People have been making buildings out of mud and clay all over the world since ancient times! Mud buildings stay cool inside and can cope with extreme weather. It's no surprise that there are entire cities of them in hot countries like Mali and Mexico. Why not think big and build an entire mini city out of air-dry clay?

List of buildings

Mini Architects © 2024 Thames & Hudson Ltd, London

Text © 2024 Joséphine Seblon
Illustrations © 2024 Robert Sae-Heng
Photographs © 2024 Thames & Hudson Ltd, London

Photography by Lauren Winsor

First published in the United States of America in 2024 by Thames & Hudson Inc., 500 Fifth Avenue, New York, New York 10110

Library of Congress Control Number 2023939929

ISBN 978-0-500-66024-9

Printed and bound in China by C & C Offset Printing Co. Ltd

Be the first to know about our new releases, exclusive content and author events by visiting
thamesandhudson.com
thamesandhudsonusa.com
thamesandhudson.com.au

To my growing children, who let me write this book when I suspect they would have rather built stuff together! A heartfelt thank you to the architects of the book: Robert and the T&H children's books team.
- J.S.

To Lottie - for your support, always. And to Joséphine for your kindness and the words that will inspire so many Mini Artists and Mini Architects.
- R.S.H.